MW01289519

Aaliyah

A Biography

By Jennifer Warner

 BOOKCAPS

BookCaps™ Study Guides
www.bookcaps.com

© 2014. All Rights Reserved.

Cover Image © Netfalls - Fotolia.com.jpg

Table of Contents

About LifeCaps

LifeCaps is an imprint of BookCaps™ Study Guides. With each book, a lesser known or sometimes forgotten life is recapped. We publish a wide array of topics (from baseball and music to literature and philosophy), so check our growing catalogue regularly (**www.bookcaps.com**) to see our newest books.

Introduction

The Dutch West Indies Company settled the
western end of Long Island in their colony of
New Netherlands in the 1600s. Bedford was a
rural community established in 1663 and it
remained an agricultural enclave for the better
part of 200 years after the English took over and
New York built up around the farms. In the mid-
1800s, the descendants of the original Dutch
settlers began selling their family lands and
Bedford and its neighbor Stuyvesant Heights,
named for Peter Stuyvesant who had been at
the head of the Dutch colony, were folded into
the ravenously growing city of Brooklyn.

One of the entrepreneurs that went on a buying spree for the old cropland was James Weeks, an African-American who carved up his new property for building lots to sell to fellow black homesteaders. Weeksville was one of the pioneering free black communities in America. By the end of the 19th century, Brooklyn was the fourth largest city in the United States, and the streets of Bedford-Stuyvesant were lined with stylish three- and four-story brownstone houses designed in the popular late Victorian styles of the day.

In the first decades of the 20th century, the United States underwent a radical demographic shift when tens of thousands of black men and women began leaving the rural South for factory jobs in the industrial North. Bedford-Stuyvesant was long known as an African-American cultural mecca around the country, and the neighborhood became a target destination for the transplants of what came to be called The Great Migration.

Unfortunately, the Great Migration was followed by the Great Depression. Bedford-Stuyvesant embarked on a long and steady economic decline. The spectacular brownstones were carved into small and overcrowded multi-family apartments and rooming houses. Those with real resources moved to the growing suburbs further out on Long Island. By the 1970s, the glory days of Bedford-Stuyvesant were long forgotten, and its only notoriety was as America's largest ghetto. In such circumstances, it required a special breed of optimism to welcome one's new daughter to the world in Bedford-Stuyvesant with the name of Aaliyah, which translates from the East African language of Swahili as "highest, most exalted one."

Chapter 1: Early Life and Influences

The parents were Diane and Michael Haughton and Aaliyah Dana Haughton was their second child, joining brother Rashad, who had been born 17 months earlier. The date was January 16, 1979. The Haughtons knew the legacy of Bedford-Stuyvesant; their ancestors in Brooklyn had worked for the nascent New York City transit authority in the early 1900s, and operated a laundry shop and a tailor shop. But in 1984, they were ready to say "good-bye."

The Haughtons packed up their young family and moved to a working class neighborhood on the west side of Detroit, Michigan. Diane's brother, Barry Hankerson, had paved the family way to Motor City by coming to Wilberforce, Ohio to play in the defensive backfield of Central State University. He dallied with a New York Jets' developmental team before giving up on football and co-founding Operation Get Down with Bernard Parker in 1971. The community-based organization worked with troubled youth and set up a transition center for homeless men as part of a substance-abuse program.

Hankerson's day job was as a local television producer, and in 1974, when Coleman A. Young became the first African-American mayor of Detroit, the 27-year old go-getter from Bedford-Stuyvesant was brought into the administration as an executive assistant. The plan was for Michael Haughton to come out from Brooklyn and work in the warehouse business that was one of Barry Hankerson's widening Detroit interests. Diane, a teacher, would stay home and raise the couple's two children, now of school age.

Aaliyah enrolled in Gesu Elementary, the local Catholic school. Gesu happened to be a very ambitious elementary school when it came to putting on its school plays which involved all ages from five through thirteen. Many of the productions were moved out of the children's auditorium and onto the stage at nearby Marygrove College on McNichols Road. In first grade, Aaliyah scored a coup by landing a part in *Annie*, playing one of the many orphans who crowded the stage. She had only one speaking line in the schoolwide production - "You're gonna get a paddle" - but she always recalled with pride the verve with which she delivered it.

Bigger parts were won as she progressed through elementary school in *42nd Street* and *Hello, Dolly*. The Broadway shows suited Aaliyah's musical sensibilities. She could sing the latest Whitney Houston hits around the house like most young girls, but she gravitated to the stars of her parents' and grandparents' era like Barbra Streisand and Sammy Davis, Jr. Stevie Wonder, Sade and Johnny Mathis were staples singing around the Haughton household - as well as Diane Haughton, who was a fine singer in her own right, and had toyed with the idea of trying it professionally. Aaliyah would later describe her musical influences by saying, "Back then those people had to do it all. They had to sing, dance and act. So that's how I was trained."

Aaliyah was not even out of grade school before she began looking at the possibilities beyond her acting troupe at Gesu Elementary and her fellow vocalists in the church choir. It was her idea at the age of nine, not her mother's, to begin making the audition rounds. It was her mother's idea, however, to drop her surname. She auditioned unsuccessfully for the television situation comedy *Family Matters* about a middle class African American family living in Chicago, but landed a chance to appear on the television talent show, *Star Search* when she was ten years old. Her devotion to tradition would manifested itself before a national audience.

The phenomenon that is the talent show on television owes its existence in part to the devastating San Francisco earthquake of 1906. Edward "Major" Bowes was a prosperous real estate man in San Francisco at the time when his empire literally collapsed beneath him. Bowles set out for New York City to start anew and found work as a composer, conductor and promoter on Broadway. With the coming of radio, Major Bowles began hosting amateur night talent shows similar to those he had managed while directing the Capitol Theatre. The *Original Amateur Hour* became a national sensation, and after Bowles died, his talent coordinator Ted Mack segued into hosting duties and carried the program to television. The contestants put their egos on the line for a grand prize of a $2000 scholarship. The final *Amateur Hour* aired in 1970.

Star Search was the direct descendant of the *Amateur Hour*, with contestants herded into eight categories of entertainment. Ed McMahon rose off of Johnny Carson's couch to assume hosting duties when the show geared up in 1983. Aaliyah made it through the audition process to appear on the televised show before the four judges in competition for the title of Star Search Teen Vocalist.

For her number Aaliyah selected a show tune from the 1937 Richard Rogers and Lorenz Hart musical *Babes in Arms*, "My Funny Valentine." The jazz standard has been interpreted on record by more than 600 artists, including Ella Fitzgerald, Frank Sinatra and Miles Davis. It was a song Aaliyah had heard her mother sing. She wore a white dress tailored by her grandmother Mintis L. Hicks Hankerson, worn in tandem with a bolero jacket; her head was a pile of curls.

Her rendition of "My Funny Valentine" did not propel her forward in the competition, leaving the 10-year old songstress in tears. It may have been a blow to the ego but scarcely career-damaging. The most successful *Star Search* alumnus to that time, Tiffany, had lost during her appearance. Britney Spears and Justin Timberlake were also summarily dismissed by the grandfatherly Ed McMahon from *Star Search*.

At the very least, her performance had made an impression on Ed McMahon. "There's a thing that you see when somebody walks on stage," McMahon recounted about the 10-year old from Detroit. "I call it 'the fire.' They got that inner fire, which has nothing to do with schooling, nothing to do with the teacher, nothing to do with the parents. There is a desire in that person to please the audience. You see enough of it to recognize it. And that's what I saw with Aaliyah."

After her near-miss on *Star Search,* the Haughtons leaned on Barry Hankerson's wide-reaching connections to advance Aaliyah's performing aspirations. Back while working as a young television producer, Hankerson had co-ordinated a telethon to benefit research into sickle cell anemia where one of the guest artists was Gladys Knight, who had broken through with her back-up group the Pips in 1966 after joining Motown Records in Detroit. The two had little to do with each other then, but a year later when Hankerson was helming a television special that featured Gladys Knight and the Pips, things were much different.

Egged on by Levi Stubbs of the Four Topps, Knight and Hankerson became involved socially despite seeming to be mismatched. Each had already been through a failed marriage; Gladys had two children and Barry one; Hankerson was a political activist in the Coleman administration, and Gladys could not pinpoint a single political cause that interested her. Nonetheless, Hankerson and Knight married in 1974 in a union that lasted until 1981.

Aunt Gladys was not only a chart-topping rhythm and blues star for Aaliyah to emulate, but the Empress of Soul also had launched her career at an early age and could pass that experience along as well. In fact, as a seven-year old from Oglethorpe, Georgia, little Gladys sang her way through the competition to win on *The Original Amateur Hour* in 1952. By the late 1980s, Knight had already received a Lifetime Achievement Award from the Rhythm & Blues Foundation. It was arranged for Aaliyah to join Gladys Knight and the Pips on stage for a week of shows in Knight's adopted hometown of Las Vegas. Aaliyah was called on stage to do a solo of "Home" from the smash hit *The Wiz* and returned to close the show with a duet of her and Knight singing "Believe in Yourself," another tune from *The Wiz*. The grade schooler from Detroit showed no traces of being intimidated by a boozy Las Vegas showroom.

In the push and pull of opposite lives that was the Gladys Knight-Barry Hankerson marriage, Knight seemed to be wielding the greater magnet; she never became very political, but he wound up deeper and deeper in show business. The conversion started early when the real life husband-and-wife went to Hollywood and made a movie together in 1976, *Pipe Dreams*.

Knight plays a Georgia girl who is offered a job on an Alaskan pipeline and Hankerson plays her philandering husband. Knight surprised with her acting prowess, and earned a Golden Globe nomination for Best Acting debut, and she would go on to appear in many more movies and television shows. His turn as Rob Wilson was Barry Hankerson's last work in front of the camera but he increasingly became involved in the cogs of the entertainment business behind the scenes.

By the 1980s, Hankerson was managing the career of the Winans, a four-brother Gospel quartet from Detroit, and he sat in as percussionist on a couple of their studio albums. In the latter half of the decade he took control of the management of Robert Sylvester Kelly, who had bounced out of a troubled youth on the streets of South Chicago. An impromptu appearance in a high school talent show led to street performing and early record deals. Using his stage name R. Kelly, he walked away with the $100,000 grand prize from yet another television talent show, *Big Break*.

Kelly and his group Public Announcement released their debut album in 1992 called *Born into the 90's* that spawned four hits with conventional rhythm and blues tracks and some hip-hop/new jack swing songs. Hankerson shared a writing credit on "She's Got That Vibe," which climbed as high as number seven on the Hot R&B charts. "Honey Love" and "Slow Dance" both clawed their way up the same charts from the album.

In 1993, R. Kelly left Public Announcement and released his first solo album, *12 Play*. It was at that time the word "genius" began being lobbed at the 26-year old singer, songwriter and producer. "Bump N' Grind" became his first number one single on the *Billboard* Hot R&B singles chart and stayed there for an unprecedented 12 weeks. "Your Body's Callin'" and Sex Me" both became gold records. As an album, *12 Play* went six times platinum.

In the new frenzy surrounding R. Kelly, his manager thought it would be a good idea for the hot phenom producer to meet his musically precocious niece. Aaliyah came into the studio and sang for Kelly, who liked what he heard enough to agree to write songs for her. Hankerson recruited his son Jomo out of his last year at Pepperdine University and formed a music recording company, Blackground Records, with Aaliyah as his first client.

Chapter 2: First Album: Age Ain't Nothing but a Number

Hankerson signed on with Jive Records to distribute his new company's records where he found a kindred soul in Clive Calder. Calder, the same age as Hankerson, was a South African bass guitarist who played in local Johannesburg bands and kept stacks of tax manuals around the house for light reading. He started his first record company in 1971 and soon launched Zomba, named for the one-time capital of the African country of Malawi. In 1981, Calder opened offices in New York City to birth Jive Records. The name emanated from a form of African dance music.

Calder became an early enthusiast of hip hop music that was beginning to take hold in New York clubs. In its first decade, Jive became the go-to label for Whodini, the trio that helped break hip hop music onto urban radio and DJ Jazzy Jeff & The Fresh Prince who came out of West Philadelphia to claim the first Grammy Award for Best Rap Performance. The new record by Aaliyah would mark Jive's diversion into a player in the rhythm and blues genre.

For her first venture into a recording studio as a signed professional artist, 14-year old Aaliyah stepped directly into the major leagues. The Chicago Recording Company (CRC) had only begun business in 1975, but what it lacked in tradition it made up for in quality. With twelve state of the art recording studios, CRC was the largest recording palace in the Midwest, and the country's biggest independent studio. Heading the list of recording artists who had polished albums at CRC was the ultimate rhythm and blues superstar, Michael Jackson.

Kelly and Aaliyah started with "Old School," singing the song over and over as the work ethic that would come to impress her collaborators was evident from the beginning. She sang in a falsetto as she searched for her sound. Later she would explain her choices by telling interviewers, "The songs came at you kind of tough, a bit edgy, hip hop, but the vocals can be very soothing."

Peter Mokran, a Chicago native who was trained in classical guitar, was working the board mixing and layering the sounds. He had broken into engineering and producing on Kelly's debut, *Born into the 90's,* and had guided the follow-up *12 Play* to its great heights. Mokran had parlayed that success into work with Janet Jackson away from his Kelly connection. By early 1994, the team had completed 14 songs for Aaliyah's debut album.

The publicity machine for the album began grinding into gear in February 1994 when Aaliyah flew to Los Angeles for the Urban Network's Power Jam V conference, a gathering of record label executives, radio men, programmers and retailers. Topics on the agenda included the role of more positive raps and encouraging R&B executives to do business with a wider variety of people to avoid becoming stagnant in the industry. Given that atmosphere, the unknown 15-year old singer from Detroit received a warm reception as she was carted around before the money men.

In May 1994, *Age Ain't Nothing But a Number* was released to the world as "written and produced by R. Kelly especially for Aaliyah." The first single, "Back & Forth," became the album's signature song when it debuted to the public on May 10. In "Back & Forth", Aaliyah sings of the anticipation of the coming weekend, and going to a party to have fun with her teenage friends.

Despite not writing the lyrics, Aaliyah could sing the song from personal experience. Despite the potential for big-timing her teenage years with a record debut with hip hop's biggest new star, Diane Haughton made sure her daughter still went to the mall for shopping with her friends, and lived as normal a life as could be expected. Aaliyah's favorite things still included hanging with her girlfriends and playing laser tag.

To support "Back and Forth", Aaliyah had shot her first music video, directed by Millicent Shelton. Shelton was a Missouri-born alumnus of Princeton University and had done graduate work at New York University's Tisch School of Arts before being tapped by director Spike Lee to work as a wardrobe assistant on his seminal 1989 film, *Do the Right Thing*. She quickly advanced into directing music videos for Salt-N-Pepa, Mary J. Blige and R. Kelly.

For the "Back and Forth" video, Shelton came to Aaliyah's hometown to film in a Detroit gym although it was not because of any clout the novice artist carried. The original shoot had been scheduled for Los Angeles, but the Northridge Earthquake that ripped through the San Fernando Valley also shook up the video production schedule. The video opens with a bounding basketball, and kids arriving and chilling in the gym. Aaliyah makes her appearance in baggy clothing, eyeshades and a bandana, singing the song. The basketball game will give way to a dance fest with many of her real-life friends, and Aaliyah spends time sitting in the bleachers with Kelly, who performs the rap in the song.

Within a month, "Back and Forth" had been certified gold and spent three weeks atop the *Billboard* Hot R&B Songs chart, and in the *Billboard* Hot 100 the single reached number five. The success of "Back and Forth" pushed the next single onto the market in August, 1994. "At Your Best (You Are Love)" was a cover of a song by the Isley Brothers that had charted in a minor way in 1976. Aaliyah's rendition peaked at number six on the *Billboard* Hot 100 and Shelton returned to film another video which was produced with another Kelly hit, "Summer Bunnies."

In November, Shelton shot a third music video from the album for the title track, "Age Ain't Nothing but a Number." The video was also produced in Detroit and Shelton used black-and-white film for the montage. The video featured the first appearance by rappers DeShaun Dupree Holton and Rufus Arthur Johnson from the local Detroit neighborhoods who would go on to become pivotal members of the hip hop group D12, the Dirty Dozen. Aaliyah's brother, Rashad, also appeared in the music video.

In 1995, two more singles were gouged out of Aaliyah's debut album, "Down with the Clique" and "The Thing I Like," neither of which dented the charts in America but made a minor stir in Great Britain. By this time, Aaliyah was on a world tour promoting her first album in Western Europe, South Africa and Japan. By the time she reached Japan, all the fans in the audience knew all the lyrics to her limited repertoire.

Age Ain't Nothing but a Number debuted at number 24 on the *Billboard* album charts and reached its greatest heights at number 18. After selling three million copies in the United States, the album was certified three times platinum. It also realized success on the Canadian, Dutch, and British charts. Critics were a bit more reserved than fans. Aaliyah was praised for her voice, but it was Kelly's songs and lush studio orchestration that generated the most buzz.

Chapter 3: Follow-Up

Record: *One in a Million*

The most buzz at least until the rumors erupted that the collaborators had been working on more than musical tracks. The racy adult-themed lyrics that Kelly was putting in teenage Aaliyah's mouth were enough to set some scold's tongues wagging, but then it started to get around that Kelly and Aaliyah had secretly married. Denials were issued all around until *Vibe* magazine published a copy of a marriage certificate that showed there was indeed a marriage at the Sheraton Gateway Suites in Rosemont, Illinois on August 31, 1994. The age given for the 15-year old Aaliyah Dani Haughton was 18.

When the facts came to light, the illegal marriage was tactfully annulled and Aaliyah's family intervened to make sure it stayed dissolved. As the careers of R. Kelly and Aaliyah both continued to arc towards stardom, she is supposed to have never seen him again. She never discusses the allegation publicly. When Kelly later pens an autobiography, Aaliyah's name is never mentioned. Each denied separately that the information in the *Vibe* article was incorrect, and both Aaliyah and Kelly would insist they were not and never were married.

In the long run, sordid talk about their relationship did not harm the careers of either Aaliyah or R. Kelly. But in the immediate aftermath, Blackground and Barry Hankerson had to put together an entire new production and distribution team for Aaliyah's follow-up album. Aside from the distractions of the tongue-wagging scandal, there was more riding on the second album than the usual curiosity about how an artist will follow a successful debut. And record distributors were not lining up to put money behind an album that did not have R. Kelly attached to it.

In the wake of *Age Ain't Nothing But a Number* Aaliyah had kick started a wave of teenage crooners, most notably Brandy Norwood and Monica Brown, each known more familiarly by her first name. As Brandy described the early days in 1994, "I was so excited to meet Aaliyah because she was the first girl on the scene. She came out before Monica and I did—she was our inspiration. At the time, record companies did not believe in kid acts and it was just inspiring to see someone that was winning, and winning being themselves."

So when Aaliyah went back into the recording studio, she would need to be convincing the music industry that she was indeed a young star of staying power, an industry that had seen the wreckage of more than its share of failed kid acts wash up against the record bins of music stores. She would not just be singing to young hip hop fans but for aspiring young hip hop artists. With all this playing out, a demo arrived in the Blackground offices called "Sugar and Spice."

The demo was from Timothy Zachery Mosley out of Norfolk, Virginia. Mosley spent his high school years as "DJ Tim" making hip hop tracks on a Casio keyboard. After coming to New York City in the early 1990s, Mosley picked up a new nickname, Timbaland, after the American manufacturer of outdoor leather boots. The Hankersons thought "Sugar and Spice" was leaning towards the kiddie side, but it did contain an intriguing triple beat that caused them to pass the song along to Aaliyah.

The 16-year old Aaliyah made her first major decision as an artist and convinced her uncle and cousin to fly Timbaland to Detroit and give him the main hand on the reins for her second album despite still being in his early twenties. Sharing songwriting duties with Timbaland was his childhood friend, Melissa Arnette "Missy" Elliott. Like Aaliyah, Elliott dreamed of a show business career beginning in her pre-school days. Her childhood was troubled by domestic abuse, however, and her entry into music was delayed until the early 1990s when she formed an R&B group with friends. Missy Elliott and her group Sista was signed by Elektra Records, and became part of a collective group of artists known as Swing Mob, all of whom were discovered by rapper and producer DeVante Swing.

After the dissolution of Swing Mob, Elliott and Timbaland teamed up as songwriting/production tandem. They were responsible for eight of the tracks that ended up on Aaliyah's sophomore outing, called *One in a Million*. Reports from the Hankerson camp suggest that 57 songs were recorded for the album on sessions conducted between August 1995 and July 1996. Other young producers working on the project who would soon make their mark in hip hop music were Rodney Jerkins, Jermaine Dupri, and Kay Gee. Also on board for several tracks was Vincent V.H. Herbert, who would work with Toni Braxton, Destiny's Child and Lady Gaga, and marry Tamar Braxton.

With his revamped production team in place, Hankerson went to look for a new record distribution deal since the revelation of the illegal marriage had voided the contract with Jive Records. He eventually hooked up with Atlantic Records. Atlantic was a legacy label with a long reputation of promoting African-American artists from jazz, rhythm and blues and soul.

With ever-more confidence, Aaliyah was also deeply involved in the project as she stood her ground for the kind of record she wanted to make. She wanted to sing about relationships, but also to create a record of different moods with plenty of party songs. Once again she covered an Isley Brothers tune, this time picking "Choosey Lover" that was a top ten R&B hit from 1983. Aaliyah performed the song in two styles which she called "Old School" and "New School", doing the first half in a manner similar to the original, and infusing the second half with a hip hop beat.

One in a Million was released on August 27, 1996 to near universal acclaim. One place the record met resistance was in the offices of radio programmers who had problems with the chirping crickets Timbaland inserted into the title track. But that was soon smoothed over. In the marketplace, the album debuted at number 20 on the *Billboard* 200 Album chart and inched its way up to a peak at number 18, exactly as *Age Ain't Nothing but a Number* had done. Like its predecessor, it was also certified double platinum within a year.

Critics were equally receptive, and it was hardly mentioned that the album had been put out without any input from her mentor R. Kelly. Aaliyah's vocal performance was observed to be stronger and smoother than on her debut album. While her seductive stylings made some uncomfortable when she was 15 years old, her singing at age seventeen was even more seductive. Even at the time of its release, *One in a Million* was being hailed as a game-changer for R&B sounds of the 1990s. By the end of the decade, *Rolling Stone* had ranked it as one of the 100 greatest albums of the 1990s, and *One in a Million* was marked as one of the 33 "essential" hip hop records that fans had to know.

One in a Million produced six singles beginning with "If Your Girl Only Knew" that was chosen to launch the record. Recorded at Pyramid Studios in Ithaca, New York, the single was a composition by Missy Elliott and Timbaland and highlighted the young Virginian's producing talents. For the music video, Hankerson once again turned to a young emerging talent, 23-year old Joseph Kahn.

Parts of Kahn's childhood were spent in South Korea and Italy before his family settled in Houston. Kahn was shooting music videos for local musicians in his teens, and after dropping out of New York University he specialized in low budget videos in Los Angeles where he worked as his own cinematographer, editor, and production designer. He did minor jobs for the likes of Willie Nelson and Public Enemy before taking on the head job for "If Your Girl Only Knew."

Kahn retained Aaliyah's trademark look of dark sunglasses and bandana and outfitted her in dark leather. She is shown in color, occupying a futuristic chair, while the party going on around her remains in black and white. Missy Elliott, Timbaland, rapper Ginuwine and Aaliyah's brother Rashad all make appearances in the video. "If Your Girl Only Knew" reached as high as number eleven on the American charts and also scored well overseas.

The next single, the title track, became a hit based on urban radio play and ruled the R&B Airplay chart for six weeks in the autumn of 1996. Aaliyah's slow soulful down tempo singing is juxtaposed against Timbaland's drum-and-bass mixing that set the song apart from the typical rhythm and blues offerings of the mid-1990s.

Aaliyah's management team had put a great deal of stock in the music video form, an art form that, by her debut in 1994, appeared to be as relevant an eight-track tapes. Even MTV had stopped showing music videos that were considered promotional relics from just a few years earlier. As videos became scarcer in the 1990s, directors' names began to be affixed to the video credits, and suddenly the quality of the three- and four-minute films began to look more polished as they attracted more accomplished camera craftsmen.

Aaliyah and the renaissance in music videos arrived at the same time, which explains the quality of the young directors in her earliest videos. Paul Hunter, who Barry Hankerson hired for the "One in a Million" video, was cut from the same cloth. He was raised in Queens where he aspired to be a painter but drifted into still photography. He traveled across the country to study film at California State University at Northridge, and almost ended up in front of the camera before concluding that an actor's life was too daunting.

His music videos cultivated a rich evocative mood which dovetailed exactly with what Aaliyah's handlers were seeking for their nascent star. The viewer is given an experience rather than a plot. The "One in a Million" music video is no exception as the camera begins by finding Aaliyah draped across the top of a black Ford Mustang. Interplay between Aaliyah and Ginuwine proceeds across atmospherically shot rooms until the song ends with Aaliyah speeding away on a motorcycle with DEALZ, a nephew of Michael Jackson.

The third single off *One in a Million* was Aailyah's cover of a chart-topping Marvin Gaye song from 1977 called "Got to Give It Up." Back then, divorce proceedings led the cash-strapped soul icon to write a disco tune which he intended as a parody. Instead, "Got to Give It Up" bounded to the top of the disco charts, the soul charts and the *Billboard* Hot 100. Michael Jackson would often credit the song as showing him the musical way after he left the Jackson 5. A converted Gaye himself traditionally used the song he intended as a throw-away to open his live shows.

Aaliyah's version was intermingled with a rap from Richard Walters, Slick Rick, and failed to gain traction in the United States, although it encouraged some minor airplay overseas. Even a music video by Paul Hunter edited with and without Slick Rick's vocals failed to excite the fans. The single's B-side did contain a rare Aaliyah composition, "No Days Go By." The fourth single, "4 Page Letter" also failed to generate much excitement; it contained a B-side written by both Aaliyah and her brother Rashad, "Death of a Playa."

"Death of a Playa" made another appearance on the album's final single that featured "Hot Like Fire" and "The One I Gave My Heart To" on the A-side. The double track single was released on September 16, 1997 and Aaliyah juiced its promotion by including "Hot Like Fire" on her set list at that year's Summer Jam. It was the singer's first appearance at the annual gathering of the most popular acts in hip hop and rhythm and blues.

Summer Jam takes place in Giants Stadium in East Rutherford, New Jersey sponsored by WQHT radio in New York City. WQHT is a heritage station that debuted in 1940 with transmitters atop the Empire State Building. By the early 1990s, the station had been floundering through a succession of formats that included news and adult contemporary and country music. With ratings at an all-time low in 1993, the station emerged as Hot 97 - Where Hip Hop Lives. By 1995, Hot 97 was the top station in New York and was a leading purveyor of urban radio; Summer Jam was launched the previous year. At Summer Jam, Aaliyah gave notice that she was not looking to be a singer but she was a performer. She took the stage in the midst of explosions and confetti showers and confidently held the stage with more than dozen dancers.

Lance "Un" Riviera was selected to direct the "Hot Like Fire" music video which would not bring him as much notoriety as two years later, when he was stabbed by rapper Jay-Z at an album release party at the Kit Kat Klub, in a dispute over a leaked bootleg copy of Jay Z's *Vol. 3...Life and Times of S. Carter.* The heat in "Hot Like Fire" is generated on a steamy summer day with sparks popping during Aaliyah's singing and dancing. Timbaland and Missy Elliott, who penned the tune, each perform their verse in the video.

"The One I Gave My Heart To" is a contrasting ballad of lament as Aaliyah wonders how she could have given her heart to a man who turned out to be such a cad. The song was written by veteran Diane Warren who, in spite of the plaintive lyrics in "The One I Gave My Heart To," claims never to have been in love like the girls in her songs. Unlike Aaliyah's previous contributors, Warren grew up far from the streets and hip hop world. She was a Jewish girl from Van Nuys, California, but like Aaliyah, she grew up wanting nothing but a career in music.

Warren's performing career languished but she spent most of her time writing songs. She scored her first hit when she was 24 years old and songstress Laura Branigan recorded "Solitaire" and it rose to number seven on the pop charts. Warren was named Pop Songwriter of the Year in 1990, 1991, and 1993 and won her first Grammy Award in 1997 for writing "Because You Loved Me" for Celine Dion.

For "The One I Gave My Heart To" Aaliyah abandoned her typical falsetto to deliver the power pop ballad, to the approval of Warren. "She could go where the Whitneys went," the songwriter gushed. "She wailed on that single I wrote for her. I write songs that challenge singers, and she rose to the occasion." "The One I Gave My Heart To" became the highest-charting single on *One in a Million*, peaking at number nine, and providing Aaliyah with another Top Ten hit.

Chapter 4: Acting

With *One in a Million,* Aaliyah had proven she was not another in a long line of one-hit wonders. Instead, she was primed to assume the mantle of the next hip hop princess. But she was in no hurry to say goodbye to her teenage years. Despite her touring and burgeoning stardom, Aaliyah did what she could to maintain a normal lifestyle. She had entered the Detroit High School of the Performing Arts at the age of 14, singing the entirety of "Ave Maria" in Latin for her audition.

While the personal bodyguard in school and the tutors were not typical of a teenage girl's existence, the collections of sunglasses and stuffed animals were. One orange orangutan named Lina was particularly dear; she was a gift from her grandmother before she passed away. It was her grandmother who had suggested Dana as her middle name. She eventually graduated from high school with a 4.0 grade point average, and attended her prom with five friends in matching suits.

One thing Aaliyah was looking forward to after graduation was to explore more acting opportunities. She had made her television debut on January 16, 1997 playing herself in the "Fade Out" episode from Season Three of *New York Undercover*. The Fox television police drama followed the adventures of a pair of detectives infiltrating and investigating crime gangs. In each episode, one of the lead players would find a way to Natalie's, a rhythm and blues cafe whose owner was played by Gladys Knight. On stage a major hip hop act would do a set. For her turn, Aaliyah performed her cover of the Isley Brothers' "Choosey Lover."

Aaliyah - or her voice - made her film debut in the animated musical fantasy feature Anastasia from 20th Century Fox studios. Anastasia tells the fable of Anastasia Nikolaevich, who was the youngest daughter of Tsar Nicholas II in July 1918 when the entire family and several servants were executed by the Bolsheviks in the Russian Revolution. Anastasia imagines the young girl surviving the bloody coup. The 1997 film was an animated remake of a live-action 1956 movie starring Ingrid Bergman and Yul Brenner.

Meg Ryan took the Bergman part providing the voice for the animated Anastasia and 36-year old Liz Callaway of Chicago provided the singing voice. The seven tunes for the musical were composed by Stephen Flaherty, with lyrics by Lynn Ahrens. Like so many of Aaliyah's collaborators, Flaherty was convinced to make music his life at an early age. By the age of 14, he had composed his first score in his hometown of Pittsburgh, and continued to pursue his music education at the Cincinnati College Conservatory.

After graduation and migration to New York City, Flaherty began studying with celebrated composer Lehman Engel, a close friend of Pablo Picasso. Engel founded the BMI Lehman Engel Musical Theater Workshop in 1961 specifically for lyricists, librettists and composers for the theater. In the early 1980s Flaherty became one of his star pupils. It is also where he met Lynn Ahrens who was raised on the Jersey Shore and educated at Syracuse University where she hoped to become a journalist before turning to songwriting. Flaherty and Ahrens began their long, award-filled collaboration in 1983.

Callaway sings a version of the song "Journey to the Past" as the Anastasia character searches for her family in the snow. When the song reappears over the closing credits, however, it is a rhythm and blues-tinged pop version from Aaliyah. The music video bounces back and forth with Aaliyah in modern America and the animated world of 1920s Russia. Critics generally preferred the in-movie version of Callaway's rather than Aaliyah's effort that was designed to be released as a single. Consumers seemed to agree as "Journey to the Past" barely tickled the Adult Contemporary charts.

At the following year's awards season, however, "Journey to the Past" picked up nominations for Best Original Song at the Academy Awards and the Golden Globes. On March 23, 1998 at the Shrine Auditorium in Los Angeles, Aaliyah became the youngest African-American female artist to perform on the live Oscar telecast that was broadcast to 57 million viewers in the United States and millions more around the globe. Her poised performance showed that she was more than ready to take the world's biggest stages as her teen years wound down. Aaliyah was denied her first Oscar by "My Heart Will Go On" from *Titanic*, the theme song of the biggest movie in history to that time. Celine Dion's biggest hit, and the best-selling single of 1998, also won the Golden Globe.

Later in 1998, Eddie Murphy attempted to recapture cinematic magic in *Dr. Dolittle* playing John Dolittle, a doctor with an ability to talk to animals. The series of children's books had produced a 1967 musical that left those involved scarred by critics' pens and at the box office. Although the re-make was a comedy marketed towards children, the soundtrack was a very adult blend of rhythm and blues and contemporary hip hop. The soundtrack album scored a major success in the music industry, peaking at number four on the *Billboard* album charts and selling more than two million copies.

Despite its great success the only song that broke out from the Dr. Dolittle soundtrack was Aaliyah's "Are You That Somebody?" The song was written by Stephen Ellis Garrett, who adopted the name Static Major. Major came out of the same Swing Mob with Ginuwine and Timbaland, but was just carving his own reputation when he showed "Are You That Somebody?" to Aaliyah. She did not like the song and had to be persuaded to record it.

Timbaland produced the cut and recorded a series of beats and loops at New York City's Hit Factory for its release as a single. He also inserted baby sounds that he dubbed from a home video of Aaliyah recorded when she was 18 months old. The rap towards the end of the song is Timbaland's. The video, directed by Santa Monica native Mark Gerard, was filmed in a cave in Griffith Park in Los Angeles, beneath the iconic "Hollywood" sign. There were two versions, one with footage from *Dr. Dolittle* projected on the walls while Aaliyah and the cast dance, and the other without the movie ties.

In addition to selling well, "Are You That Somebody?" benefited by a change in *Billboard* policy to incorporate radio airplay into its chart calculations. With that bump Aaliyah soon topped the Hot R&B/Hip Hop Airplay chart and rocketed to number four on the Hot 100 Airplay chart with "Are You That Somebody?" Overseas, the song was a hit as well. Aaliyah had always done well on the Dutch music charts, and this became one of her best-selling records in the Netherlands ever. "Are You That Somebody?" went to number one and stayed on the Dutch charts for 22 weeks.

In 1999, Aaliyah was nominated for a Grammy for Best Female R&B Vocal on "Are You That Somebody?" The music video copped an NAACP Image Award Nomination for Outstanding Music Video. Back at the Shrine Auditorium for the Grammy Awards on February 24, 1999, 20-year old Aaliyah was joined in the category for Best Female R&B Vocal Performance by legends Aretha Franklin, who had won 18 Grammys, and Janet Jackson, whose credits included over 140 million records sold. All were bested that year by Lauryn Hill, who was riding the crest of her debut album, *The Miseducation of Lauryn Hill*.

Aaliyah's fashion sense came naturally. Her mother suggested that she hide one eye behind her bangs to give her look an allure, but otherwise she just wore her favorite baggy pants and tops and the rest of the teen world followed behind. In her early teen years, she expressed a disdain for skirts and dresses, but she eventually grew out of that tomboy phase of her personality. It happened all of a sudden when she looked in the mirror and concluded that her saggy look made her appear like an oversized child.

The covered-eye look was inspired by femme fatale Veronica Lake from 1940s Hollywood who happened to be Diane Haughton's all-time favorite actress. When Aaliyah adopted the style to go along with her preference for dark glasses the rumor mill kicked into overdrive. Aaliyah has a lazy eye! Aaliyah has crossed eyes! Aaliyah has a glass eye (Aliyah's all-time favorite rumor about herself that percolated out of fan magazines!) As the rumors grew even crazier, Aaliyah began switching her hair style to cover her left eye on some days and the right days on others. Instead of fans catch on the rumors changed to "Aaliyah has problems with both eyes!" The only condition the hip hop idol ever suffered from was a fondness for sunglasses.

By 1998 she had signed an endorsement contract with the Tommy Hilfiger Corporation. Tommy Hilfiger was born in Elmira, New York and started to work in retail after leaving high school. In the early 1970s, Hilfiger would travel into New York City, gather up the latest styles of jeans and bell-bottom pants and bring them back to Elmira to sell. He later started designing clothing for his accounts, and eventually moved to New York City to become a designer. Hilfiger turned down offers from established designers like Calvin Klein and Perry Ellis to try and make a go of it as an independent.

He founded the Tommy Hilfiger Corporation in 1984, and took the company public in 1992 as he became an early player in the arena of lifestyle marketing. He started by sponsoring rock-and-roll tours including Pete Townshend, but his deal with Aaliyah help seal his leadership position in urban culture. Hilfiger featured Aaliyah in his Summer Fashion show in Jamaica in 1998, playing up her trademark image of "street but sweet" and introducing sagging pants to millions of women. In the ads, Aaliyah was seen wearing men's boxer shorts under baggy jeans with a tight tube top. For Hilfiger, it was an entirely new look, sexy, yet somehow classic.

Over the years, Hilfiger lined up a stable of celebrities to wear Tommy gear but none slid more perfectly into Tommy Jeans than Aaliyah, who was now being called Baby Girl by her fans, in a series of print ads and commercials for the brand. At one Tommy Hilfiger Fashion Show, Aaliyah met Kidada Jones, a daughter of music impresario Quincy Jones, and the two became linked in the gossip magazines as "best friends."

Several years older than Aaliyah, the two shared the same tastes in music, fashion, and fun. As Jones became more trusted by the family, she replaced Michael or Diane as guardian on a European Aaliyah tour. The two clubbed and shopped their way from gig to gig as Aaliyah transitioned from teenager to adult in the public eye.

In 1999, *Teen People* magazine named Aaliyah one of its "21 Hottest Stars Under 21" as she was also making the transition from music to movies. By this time, she had appeared in ten music videos when she was cast in the lead female role for Warner Brothers' production of *Romeo Must Die,* which was billed as a hip-hop Kung-Fu action movie based on the Shakespeare tragedy of Romeo and Juliet. Aaliyah would not be the only rookie on the set.

Andrzej Bartkowiak was approaching his 50th birthday having made his Hollywood reputation as cinematographer on a string of Hollywood hits including *The Verdict*, *Twins*, *Speed*, and *Lethal Weapon 4*. For his first job as a director, Bartkowiak not only had an untried actress in his female lead, but a non-English speaker in the male lead, Jet Li. Jet Li was a martial arts national champion in China and veteran of more than twenty Hong Kong films before making his American debut in 1998's *Lethal Weapon 4*.

When the cast of newcomers required a voice of experience, Delroy Lingo was on hand to share his background acting in *Clockers*, *Get Shorty*, *Ransom* and a host of other productions. Big-time Hollywood producer Joel Silver was given a $25 million budget and production was set for studios in North Vancouver in British Columbia, Canada.

Romeo Must Die spends less time on Romeo's romancing and most of its screen time on the dying part. There is very little romance and no sex scenes for Aaliyah's big screen debut, but she does get one fight scene as Trish O'Day. The movie would garner mixed critical reviews, but those fight scenes were well regarded, with the bar fight picking up a nomination for a Taurus Award from the World Stunt Awards for its six performers and sheets of breaking glass.

For her part, Aaliyah showed enough promise in her acting debut to begin fueling speculation over her next part. "I like acting and enjoyed making this. I really want to get into it. I'm looking for my next movie now," she told fans. She was nominated by the MTV Movie Awards for Best Female Performance and Breakthrough Female Performance. She was also nominated as Best Actress for the Black Entertainment Television Awards.

In addition to performing as lead actress, Aaliyah was also listed as executive producer for the *Romeo Must Die* soundtrack, and she ended up cutting four of the 18 tracks on the album. The production team actually plotted out the soundtrack, featuring artists such as Blade, Mack 10, Destiny's Child and Dave Hollister, before crafting the movie. Although there were few standouts on the compilation, the record reached the top of the R&B Album charts and karate-chopped its way all the way to number three on the *Billboard* 200 album charts.

A promotional single, "I Don't Wanna" was released in 1999 prior to the movie and reached number 35 on the *Billboard* Hot 100. It was the first charting effort from Darnley Scantlebury, known professionally as Donnie Scantz, who also produced the track with Kevin Hicks. The first single released off the soundtrack was "Try Again," a composition by Timbaland and Static Major. The single revolutionized measurements of success in the music industry when it became the first song ever to ascend to number one on the *Billboard* Hot 100 based only on its air play.

Timbaland kicked off the record with a tribute to Eric B. & Rakim, the most influential DJ/MC combo of the 1980s, and one of the most revered hip hop duos of all time, by rapping the opening verse to "I Know You Got Soul" from their 1987 release of *Paid in Full*. The song was recognized by *Rolling Stone* as one of the 500 Greatest Songs of All Time.

Laid down against Timbaland's echoing soundscape, Aaliyah's hypnotic vocals and chord manipulation carry the remainder of the track, causing *The New York Times* to conclude, "'Try Again' helped smuggle the innovative techniques of electronic dance music onto the American pop charts, and it established Aaliyah as pop music's most futuristic star."

Wayne Isham, one of the few music video directors whose career dated back to the earliest days of MTV, took charge of the music video for "Try Again." He had worked with the likes of Bon Jovi and Motley Crue and Ozzy Osbourne, and just as Timbaland opened the song with an homage, Isham started the video with an homage to the greats of film. Jet Li enters a hall of mirrors first used by Orson Welles in 1948's *Lady from Shanghai* and then mimicked by Woody Allen in *Manhattan Murder Mystery* and Bruce Lee in *Enter the Dragon*.

"Come Back in One Piece" was the third single to be released from the soundtrack of *Romeo Must Die*. It had actually circulated with "I Don't Wanna" and did not do much business in the United States. It is notable mostly for the guest appearance of Earl Simmons, DMX, who had just broken through with a best-selling album *...And Then There Was X* and had a role in *Romeo Must Die* as Silk. He also appears in the music video for "Come Back in One Piece" where scenes from the movie play on a television. Aaliyah shares screen time not only with DMX but also her dog in a gritty video shot in Yonkers, New York.

"Try Again" earned Aaliyah her second Grammy nomination for Best Female R&B Vocal Performance but this time she lost out to Toni Braxton who took home her fourth Grammy. "Try Again" was nominated for Song of the Year at the Lady of Soul Awards but came up short against gospel artist Yolanda Adams. Aaliyah did prevail at the MTV Video Awards for Best Female Video taking down Britney Spears, Braxton, Christina Aguilera and Macy Gray. The music video from *Romeo Must Die* also won for Best Video from a Film at the MTV back-slapping fest that year.

Aaliyah barely had time to bask in her big screen movie debut before she was back at work in the movies for Warner Brothers. She was the first actor cast in the upcoming production of *Queen of the Damned*, a vampire yarn based on the Vampire Chronicles created by Anne Rice. Warner Brothers had the rights to the first three Rice novels and had scored a hit with the first one, *Interview with the Vampire*, starring Tom Cruise in 1994.

According to the contract the studio had until the year 2000 to put the other two novels into production or the rights would revert back to Rice. As the century drew to a close that appeared to be what would happen until a last-minute script was cobbled from the two remaining books by a television movie-screenwriter Scott Abbott and an Australian director named Michael Petroni. The plot involved the vampire protagonist Lestat being awakened from a protracted sleep by the wailing of a heavy metal band, which he ends up fronting, and becoming an international rock star.

Lestat in turn awakens the original vampire, Queen Akasha, which drives an increasingly twisted plot. After Aaliyah was cast the hunt was on to find an actor to portray Lestat, the role assumed previously by Cruise. The producers eventually landed on Stuart Townsend, a 28-year old Irish actor who was primarily a stage actor but had begun attracting notice in small films. *Queen of the Damned* would be his first appearance in a big budget movie.

Another Australian, Michael Rymer. was hired to direct. His biggest project to date had been *In Too Deep*, a crime thriller with Omar Epps and LL Cool J in the leads. Rymer explained why Aaliyah had been cast so quickly, "There were two factors for casting Aaliyah. I was very keen that Akasha, an Egyptian queen, not look like Elizabeth Taylor in *Cleopatra*. And not only did she do a good job on *Romeo Must Die*, but people came to see *her*. This is a really difficult role and she took on a huge challenge. She worked her ass off for this film."

That work involved a personal trainer and a stunt coordinator to prep her for scenes in which she is called upon to fly. She also worked with Joanne Baron, a personal acting coach who had tutored a young Halle Berry and Patrick Dempsey, and spent a month with a speech coach in New York City. To save some money from the $35 million budget, it was decided to film in Australia, and shooting commenced on October 2, 2000 in the suburbs of Melbourne, using a studio converted from a one-time biscuit factory. The capital of the state of Victoria was used for location shots and an old quarry used to stand in for Death Valley where Lestat puts on a pivotal concert in the movie. Producers scoured local clubs and youth haunts to find 3,000 extras dressed as Goths for the scene.

In only her second picture, Aaliyah had made the complete transition from singing sensation to movie star. Even though the plot of *Queen of the Damned* was carried by the vampire Lestat's adventures as a rock music star, Aaliyahd had no singing to do in the movie. She also contributed nothing to the soundtrack. She was also able to throw enough influence around to get a dear friend into the movie: Lina, the stuffed orange orangutan given to her by her grandmother.

In fact, even as she worked on *Queen of the Damned,* Aaliyah was already booked for a string of additional movies. She had the lead role in *Honey* about a young woman who toils as a bartender, record store clerk and a dance teacher while dreaming of breaking into music videos. Cameos and performances by popular hip hop stars were sprinkled through the movie. There was also talk of Aaliyah starring in a remake of the 1976 drama, *Sparkle*, that was loosely based on the Supremes but set in Harlem in the 1950s.

While those were natural features to include Aaliyah, she had also been cast by producer Joel Silver to play the role of Zee in the two sequels to the massive hit *The Matrix*. There was no singing for her part in *The Matrix Reloaded* which started shooting in 2001.

Chapter 5: Third Album:
Aaliyah

Not that Aaliyah was neglecting her music career as she established herself as a Hollywood actress. She had not released an album of her own songs since 1996, and had purposely cut back her musical appearances to avoid early overexposure, but nonetheless had been working towards the third album since 1998. She collected material recorded with Blackground's writers and producers when she could in studios in New York City and Los Angeles.

She recorded two songs with go-to producer Timbaland but she also began reaching out beyond her familiar crew. She contacted Trent Reznor of Nine Inch Nails, a long-time alternative musical hero, to collaborate on a song but schedules could not be made to mesh. Aaliyah had targeted 1999 for her third album to be released, but by 2000 it was still not materializing, so she started recording songs in Australia. Days were spent playing an Egyptian vampire queen and nights were spent in Sing Sing Studios on Gordon Street in downtown Melbourne. Her cousin Jomo, now elevated to president of his father's Blackground Records, joked that he had to bribe the company producers to fly "halfway around the world" to find Aaliyah, but the 15 tracks for the album eventually came together.

Meanwhile James "Jimmy Henchman" Rosemond was put in charge of tracking down songwriters and material. Jimmy Henchman, stemming from a Brooklyn background, was so well connected to the hip hop world as head of his Czar Entertainment that the *New York Times* would describe him as "a prince at the royal court, whose ties to rap music's biggest stars were known far and wide." Those connections went beyond hooking up recording artists with songwriters, as Rosemond was eventually convicted of drug trafficking and sentenced to life imprisonment.

Lyric writing for the songs proved to be an easier chore. Since the acclaim lavished on the singles "Are You That Somebody?' and "Try Again" Major Static had migrated to the core of Aaliyah's inner working circle. Of all the lyricists that came to work for Aaliyah none captured her "street but sweet" vibe like Static who was able to infuse the songs with an alluring sexuality without being overtly offensive.

As executive producer on her third album, Aaliyah was also looking to strike a balance musically. She wanted to give her fans the rhythm and blues stylings they had come to love while also expanding her musical education. She brought in Stephen Anderson, who had become a prominent hip hop producer of the West Coast sound as Bud'da. He had been a lead producer for Westside Connection, featuring Ice Cube, Mack 10 and WC, on their debut album *Bow Down* which had helped raise the California sound to prominence. Bud'da would write and produce three songs for Aaliyah for this outing.

While her first album was mostly an R. Kelly production and her second effort a Timbaland creation, the diverse strands of Aaliyah's third album came together in Bernie Grundman Mastering in Hollywood. Grundman had been chief mastering engineer at A&M Records since the 1960s before opening his own studio in 1984. In the years that followed, Grundman became an integral link in the music created by a broad range of genres from Michael Jackson to Alanis Morissette to Dr. Dre to Joni Mitchell.

On the publicity tour to promote the self-titled *Aaliyah,* she expressed her pleasure in the finished product. "This album is a good reflection of Aaliyah and the person she is today," said the singer, adopting the use of the third person. "I am a young adult now, and I think this album shows my growth vocally. Even if the feel of it is older, it is still something my younger fans can relate to. I am very happy with it. It has something for everybody."

The first single to drop off of Aaliyah was "We Need a Resolution" on April 13, 2001. The theme of the album was a celebration of relationships - good, bad and worse. The song by Timbaland and Major Static speaks to a couple with unresolved issues in their relationship, and the yearning of the woman voiced by Aaliyah to break down the barriers of non-communication. In the song's featured rap, Timbaland laughs off the concerns of his mate, adding to her angst.

Paul Hunter was called back to direct the music video for "We Need a Resolution." He opened the vignette with Aaliyah sitting in a a dark room and by the end, after appearances by Timbaland and a bevy of dancers, she is still in a dark room, her relationship issues as unresolved as ever. Receiving almost as much screen time in the video as Aaliyah was a massive reticulated python. During the filming of *Queen of the Damned* she had occasion to act with several pythons and discovered, after initial trepidation, that she quite liked the interactions. So when it came time to shoot her new album's first video she incorporated one her new-found reptile friends into the production.

Naturally, the massive python wrapped around the sultry songstress attracted attention and led observers to conclusions about her ability to charm the phallic creatures. But to Aaliyah, snakes were a representation not of carnality, but of her mysterious side. As she told an interviewer, "They're very mysterious creatures. They live in solitude. There are times in my life I just want to be by myself. There are times I can't even figure myself out. I feel they are very complex creatures. At the same time, they're sexy, too. That's why they represent Aaliyah pretty well. They're dangerous, but quite beautiful. I thought that it would be an animal that could represent me on this album, so I wanted to take it from the photo shoot to the video and probably throughout the whole project."

The pythons became part of her promotional cycle for the record. When Aaliyah showed up for an appearance on MTV they wanted her to show up with a live python. Blackground Associate Michelle Cramer was sent scurrying to a local pet store to obtain a python, but the store only had little baby snakes. The python she brought back made its television debut curled around Aaliyah's wrist and not wrapped around her body. She kept the baby python as a pet in her Manhattan condo on Central Park West for awhile before it became too much of a responsibility, and gave the reptile away.

"We Need a Resolution" went into heavy rotation on the radio and the video became a staple of the music cable networks but the single did only moderate business worldwide. The single peaked at only number 59 on the *Billboard* 100. A few months later in July, Aaliyah's first album as an adult was released. It sold 187,000 copies in its first week, the best business Aaliyah had ever done in a week's time, and debuted at number two on the *Billboard* 200 album charts. But after that, the brisk early sales settled to such a degree that *Aaliyah* was underperforming *One in a Million*.

The self-titled *Aaliyah* received the best reviews of the rhythm and blues singer's young career. Most critics noted her new maturity as she progressed from her teen performances to more nuanced presentations. Others pointed out that a newly confident Aaliyah was showing off her vocals more and relying less on electronic enhancement and wizardry. Even the less glowing overall reviews found something to be positive about on *Aaliyah,* which was moving the singer towards a more mid-tempo sound than the club beats that had defined her first two albums.

Chapter 6: Death

Despite a budding Hollywood acting career and a steady edging towards musical superstardom, Aaliyah had found time to participate in a social life. Unlike other teen idols, she never spoke about her personal life in interviews, as might be expected from someone who most people heard about for the first time as a supposed underage child bride. While that episode might have crushed other teenagers, by the time she was 21 it was a rarely mentioned footnote in Aaliyah's career.

She was often linked romantically with her collaborators and fan magazines latched on to whatever snippets about their idol's life leaked out. "Aaliyah's first kiss a disaster - she threw up in the guy's mouth!" "Aaliyah thinks Larenz Tate is fine!" "Aaliyah loves to sing Donny Hathaway in the shower!"

In the summer of 2000, the accountant of 29-year old hip hop mogul Damon Dash introduced him to Aaliyah. Dash had grown up in Harlem where he swept hair off barbershop floors and peddled newspapers on street corners to earn money. In 1992, Dash met a young rapper named Jay-Z, and four years later the pair formed a production company with silent partner Kareem "Biggs" Burke called Roc-A-Fella Records. Jay-Z's first album, *Reasonable Doubt*, became a smash hit, and the Roc-A-Fella empire was on its way to include designer clothes, top-of-the-line vodka, books and movies. It was thus appropriate that the young hip hop mogul would be introduced to Aaliyah by an accountant since one was never far from the entourage.

The couple began as friends, but romance bloomed despite the difficulties of hectic schedules and Aaliyah's being away for months at a time. By the summer of 2001, with filming on *Queen of the Damned* completed and *Aaliyah* released, the couple looked forward to their first real stretch of spending time together. There was even talk of marriage.

Executives at Blackground, however, were perplexed at the performance of *Aaliyah*. Despite the enthusiastic reviews and the initial burst of sales the album was not taking off as hoped, especially in the offices of Richard Branson's Virgin Records who had partnered with Blackground on distribution. What was needed was a high-charting music video to bring attention back to the album.

The first song to be targeted for high-powered video treatment was "More Than a Woman," a club-influenced effort by Timbaland where Aaliyah delivers Major Static's lyrics over the clashing of synthesizers and guitar riffs. Without the production Aaliyah appeared on *Live with Regis & Kathy* on July 18 and a week later sang the song on *The Tonight Show with Jay Leno*. The music video was scheduled to be shot in early August in California following the *Tonight Show* appearance.

Dave Meyers was tabbed to direct the music video for "More Than a Woman." Meyers would go on to create over 200 music videos and win awards for his work with Pink, Alicia Silverstone and Britney Spears but in August of 2001 his main claim to fame was directing the hip hop comedy club feature, *Foolish*, which was an Eddie Griffin vehicle in 1999. In "More Than a Woman" Aaliyah co-stars with a Triumph Speed Triple motorcycle, doing wheelies and dancing almost with the bike as a partner. Real-life cohorts included Aaliyah's best friend Kidada Jones and her sister Rashida Jones, who would later star in the long-running situation comedy, *Parks and Recreation*. Also in the cast was Mark Ronson, a British music producer who would be a future Grammy winner and paramour of Rashida Jones.

When filming of "More Than a Woman" ended, Aaliyah flew to Miami to begin shooting another music video for the single "Rock the Boat," the first single released from the album written and produced by Eric Seats and Rapture Stewart, who provided seven tracks on *Aaliyah*. Rapture had been part of Keybeats that had done shows with Playa, Ginuwine and Timbaland. He wound up doing songs for *Romeo Must Die* but none with Aaliyah. She was impressed with the songs Rapture provided for Destiny's Child, Chante Moore and Dave Hollister in the movie and arranged for Blackground to bring him on board for *Aaliyah*.

Like most of the tracks from Seats and Rapture, most of the work for "Rock the Boat" was completed in 1999 before Aaliyah got deeply into her movie work. Static Major's sensual lyrics have its female narrator instructing a lover on the fine art of pleasure which suggested a nautical theme as metaphor to music video director Hype Williams. Shooting began with a nine-hour marathon in a Miami soundstage and then a follow-up in a local outdoor pool for underwater scenes.

The next day, the crew and 15,000 pounds of production equipment commanded three planes to fly to the Bahamas to continue shooting on the secluded private beaches of the Treasure Cay Resort. Dance scenes were shot on the *Fat Cat*, a private yacht almost as long as a basketball court. Williams utilized aerial and tracking shots of Aaliyah walking on a beach. The video also included a computer generated scene of Aaliyah appearing to dance on water. The choreography was provided by Fatima Robinson, longtime dance coordinator for Aaliyah music videos. Shooting wrapped up on "Rock the Boat" on August 25, 2001 and Aaliyah and her crew packed up and headed for home.

Aaliyah and seven members of her entourage lifted off from Marsh Harbour International Airport on Abaco Island at 6:45 p.m. headed for Opa-Locka Airport northwest of Miami, eager to make connections to California and New York. The original charter was scheduled for Sunday morning, but Aaliyah wanted to return to New York City as soon as possible to prepare for an upcoming stint as a presenter for the MTV Awards. Just 200 feet beyond the runway, the Cessna 402B plunged to earth and exploded on impact. Six of the nine people on board, including Aaliyah, died in the crash; none of the other three survived the day.

An autopsy of the pilot, 30-year old Luis Morales III, indicated that he had traces of alcohol and cocaine in his bloodstream. Less than three weeks earlier he had been pulled over for running a stop sign in Pompano Beach, Florida and pleaded no contest to a felony charge for cocaine possession. His plea rendered him not authorized to fly the plane for Blackhawk International Airways. Despite that damning evidence, initial suspicions were that the plane had been improperly loaded.

The Cessna wreckage was hauled to a hangar at Mount Harbour International Airport and a joint investigation begun by the Royal Bahamas Police Force, the islands' Civil Aviation Department, the Federal Aviation Administration and the National Transportation Safety Board. An official coroner's inquest two days later revealed that the 22-year old R&B singer died from severe burns and a blow to the head. It was noted that she suffered from a weak heart and shock would have prevented any recovery had she survived the crash.

The preliminary findings by the investigators were released within two weeks and confirmed original suspicions. "The total weight of the luggage, fuel on board at the time of the accident, plus the weight of the passengers showed that the total gross weight of the airplane was substantially exceeded," the report indicated. No mechanical problems were found in the engines or body of the twin-engine plan. It was noted that Morales was expecting to pick up only five passengers but allowed all eight to board.

Funeral Services were arranged by the Frank E. Campbell Funeral Chapel on Madison Avenue in Manhattan. Frank Ellis Campbell had practically invented the public funeral service in America after becoming a mortician in 1898. At the time, funerals were almost exclusively the province of the family's own private parlor. Campbell constructed a million-dollar funeral palace at Broadway and 66th Street in 1915 and outfitted the interior with precious hardwoods and tapestries said to have belonged to the Emperor Napoleon himself. New York's wealthy upper crust soon came to demand a farewell from the exclusive second-floor Gold Room in the Frank E. Campbell Funeral Chapel. Campbell even employed a press agent full time.

The famous soon joined the rich in expecting a Campbell funeral service after he orchestrated the funeral for silent film star Rudolph Valentino in 1926 for an estimated 100,000 mourners. Over the years, Campbell's became the choice for star funerals whether they were private affairs such as those held for John Lennon and Jacqueline Kennedy Onassis, or public farewells such as were staged for Judy Garland.

The private funeral and church service for Aaliyah took place on the morning of August 28, 2001. In addition to the family, Missy Elliott, Sean Combs, Busta Rhymes, Lil' Kim, Usher, Jay-Z and Chris Rock were among the mourners. The silver-plated and copper casket was transported from the funeral home three blocks to Park Avenue and the St. Ignatius Loyola Church in a glass-encased, white carriage drawn by two white horses. Following the church service, 22 white doves, one for each of Aaliyah's years, were released into the sky. Diane Haughton sent the first dove away on its journey from a white wicker box while standing in front of the coffin.

The casket was transported by hearse to its final resting place in Ferncliff Cemetery and Mausoleum in Hartsdale, New York, about 25 miles north of Midtown Manhattan in Westchester County. Established in 1902 Ferncliff features three community mausoleums that have become the final resting place for scores of actors, musicians and celebrities. The first, known as The Cathedral of Memories opened in 1928, and was followed by the Shrine of Memories in 1956. The Rosewood Mausoleum was fabricated in 1999 by skilled artisans integrating elegant marbles and granites into the surrounding landscape. Aaliyah was interred in a private room in Rosewood; Unit 4A Tier CC Private Section, Crypt 3.

Two public memorial services were scheduled to allow Aaliyah's core fan base of teenage girls and young women to say goodbye. On August 31, the magnificent interior space at Cipriani's restaurant at 110 East 42nd Street in New York City that was once the headquarters of the Bowery Savings Bank was transformed into a shrine for fans to visit and leave remembrances from 10:00 a.m until 8:00 p.m. The marble and limestone walls designed by Edward York and Philip Sawyer, the city's outstanding bank architects of the early 20th century, were lined with candles while two large television monitors played Aaliyah performances and videos on a continuous loop. The line to enter the vaulted Romanesque entrance stretched two blocks and an estimated 5,000 fans paid their respects.

In Detroit, a candlelight vigil was held at the High School of Fine and Performing Arts where many who knew their fellow graduate were able to leave flowers and stuffed animals as a farewell. Statements were read from many in the R&B community, and posters and cards were spread around the school grounds with personal messages.

Chapter 7: Posthumous Career

While she did everything she could to limit her exposure during her brief career, there would be no such parsing of her appearances in the Aaliyah posthumous career. In the immediate aftermath of the announcement of her death sales of *Aaliyah* climbed 41.5 percent and the following week exploded another fivefold taking the album to the top of the *Billboard* 200 from its pre-plane crash position of number 19. It was Aaliyah's first number one album and the first by any artist to go to the number one position posthumously since John Lennon's *Double Fantasy* twenty years earlier. Less than one month after her death *Aaliyah* passed the one million mark for units sold.

The singles "More Than a Woman" and "Rock the Boat" were rushed into rotation before the end of the year. *Queen of the Damned* was released in February of 2002 and topped the box office on its opening weekend, taking in over $15 million. The producers used Aaliyah's brother Rashad to voice a couple of scenes in post-production, and dedicated the film to her memory. Following a prolonged audition process, Nona Gaye, daughter of Marvin Gaye, was cast in the role of Zee in the Matrix movies, although Aaliyah's already-shot footage was preserved for inclusion on extras of the DVD.

When the 2002 awards season rolled around, Aaliyah won a National Association for the Advancement of Colored People (NAACP) Image Award for Outstanding Female Artist in her first nomination. At the 29th American Music Awards produced by Dick Clark on January 9, she beat out Mary J. Blige and Alicia Keys as Favorite Soul/R&B Female Artist, an honor she had been denied in her first nomination in 1999. Aaliyah also won as Favorite Soul/R&B Album of the year in 2001.

At the Grammy Award ceremonies the following month, *Aaliyah* was nominated for Best R&B Album, and Aaliyah picked up a nomination for Best R&B Vocal Performance for "Rock the Boat." She was bested by newcomer Alicia Keys in both categories. In 2003, Aaliyah would be Grammy-nominated for the fourth time for "More Than a Woman", since it was not released until early 2002. Aaliyah would be denied a Grammy for the final time when she lost out to Mary J. Blige's "He Think I Don't Know."

The inevitable compilation album arrived before 2002 was out, *I Care 4 U*, issued by Blackground Records and distributed by Universal Music. The fourteen tracks were a smorgasbord of "greatest hits" and six previously unreleased songs and demos from Aaliyah's studio sessions. *I Care 4 U* peaked when it debuted on the *Billboard* 200 charts at number three, but remained atop the R&B/Hip Hop Album Chart for seven consecutive weeks. Eventually 1.7 million copies were sold as the album was certified Platinum.

The first single was "Miss You," recorded four years earlier but never released by Blackground, which saw no potential for "smash record" status in the song. "Miss You" was a collaboration among Ginuwine, Teddy Bishop and Johnta Austin. Austin had started his show business career even earlier than Aaliyah, when he hosted a daily television show on CNN called *Kid's Beat* when he was only eight years old in 1989. Bishop, who studied recording engineering at the Detroit Institute of the Arts, handled the producing chores. The song was originally targeted for a Ginuwine album, but after Aaliyah heard it at Manhattan Center Studios, she asked to do a version of it as well.

"Miss You" missed its ride on *100% Ginuwine* and did not surface until Aaliyah's compilation album. It quickly charted in countries around the world when released on November 16, 2002, and topped the Hot R&B/Hip Hop Songs chart. When "Miss You" grabbed the number three slot on the *Billboard* Hot 100 it became the biggest hit for Aaliyah since "Try Again" had went to number one in 2000.

Darren Grant, a veteran of more than four score R&B and hip hop music videos directed the music video for "Miss You" that was essentially a tribute to the late singer from former friends and collaborators appearing with her vocals in the background. "Miss You" would be nominated in 2003 for Best R&B Video at the MTV Video Music Awards where it was nudged out by Beyoncé and Jay-Z and "Crazy In Love."

The title track was a pillow of a ballad written by Missy Elliott and Timbaland for 1996's *One in a Million*. It was left off that album but found its way onto the self-titled *Aaliyah*. "I Care 4 U" was sent into the midst of Aaliyah fandom as a single in April of 2003 and performed well as a radio song, living for 20 weeks on the Hot 100 Airplay charts and keeping the Aaliyah sound alive as a fresh radio presence.

"Don't Know What to Tell Ya" greeted the summer of 2003. Composed by Timbaland with words from Major Static, the track was recorded for the final studio album but ultimately did not make it on the record. "Don't Know What to Tell Ya" has Aaliyah counseling her new lover that she is not the devious player his former girlfriend was. It achieved mild success in the United Kingdom and Germany, where a music video directed by Bill Schacht cut archived scenes from former videos into the beat of the song was also released.

"Come Over," another song by Johnta Austin, was the last single to be released from *I Care 4 U*. Also previously unreleased, it hit the charts as fresh Aaliyah music, and did well on heavy radio rotation during the summer of 2003. It became the last Top Ten Aaliyah single when it peaked at number nine. It would be the last original Aaliyah music to appear on American airwaves.

The Aaliyah musical catalog was mined by Blackground for the final time in 2005 with a compilation package called *Ultimate Aaliyah* that was released in Great Britain, Australia and Japan. *Ultimate Aaliyah* contains one musical disc highlighting her greatest hits and another called *Are You Feelin' Me* that culls material from movie soundtracks. The package also includes a 60-minute DVD called *The Aaliyah Story* that tells the singer's tale through interviews, news clips and promotional pieces. The title cut of *Are You Feelin' Me* was released as a promotional single in the United Kingdom but never cracked the charts. Aaliyah still had enough pulling power four years after her death to generate sales of 1.4 million copies of *Ultimate Aaliyah* around the world.

But that would be it, unlike other deceased musicians whose every scrap of music often finds its way into the public. Aaliyah's family dealt with managing her memory much as they had her life and career, striving to avoid exploitation. The Haughtons filed negligence suits against Blackhawk and Virgin Records over the plane crash that took their daughter's life, but settled quietly out of course rather than replay the tragedy in the press. They did not release every last studio recording made by Aaliyah, and there were no home movies put on the market.

As the years rolled by, far from receding from the public view Aaliyah's legend only grew, and her life as a public figure began to trump any efforts of the Haughtons to protect her legacy. As the ten-year anniversary of her death approached, a documentary entitled *Aaliyah Live in Amsterdam* was released in the Netherlands, always one of the hottest markets for the rhythm and blues stylist.

Pogus Caesar, a West Indies-born artist who became a famed British television presenter, obtained access to Aaliyah's first world tour promoting her debut album *Age Ain't Nothing but a Number* in 1995. He did so merely by requesting an interview, a ploy that would soon be impossible in Aaliyah's skyrocketing career. In addition to rare live footage of the Netherlands leg of the tour at the Escape Club in Amsterdam, Caesar shot interviews with both the 16-year old Aaliyah and her father, Michael. The 52-minute film had its premiere in Caesar's hometown of Birmingham, England in the summer of 2011.

Using his personal footage, Caesar was able to create his movie without contacting the family, who likely did not know such footage existed. Not that there was anything to object to, as Caesar had held onto the increasingly valuable early footage for 15 years and never attempted to exploit its existence during Aaliyah's rise to stardom, or in the wake of her tragic death. The line between respect and exploitation would not be so finely drawn in upcoming projects.

Rumors of supposedly previously lost Aaliyah tracks recorded by producer Jeffrey "J. Dub" Walker began surfacing, and in 2012 Rashad Haughton was forced to release a statement via Twitter that declared that "no official album is being released and supported by the Haughton family." Meanwhile, Aubrey Drake Graham, a Canadian rapper who was not yet known as Drake as 14-year old when Aaliyah died, was becoming one of hip hop's hottest stars. He made it known that despite the presence of big-name male rappers, Aaliyah had been the biggest influence on his music. He went so far as to tattoo her face on his back and get her birth date inked on his rib cage.

He also announced plans to "record" a track with the late singer and inserted vocals previously unheard with a new verse of his own into the single "Enough Said," bringing new Aaliyah music to the airwaves 11 years after her death. When the single was released, Drake also began promoting the notion of a new posthumous Aaliyah project that he would be producing with unreleased tracks and fragments of songs.

The family immediately denounced the plans for such an album, and familiar voices inside the Aaliyah camp such as Timbaland and Missy Elliott quickly announced they had no intentions of being part of any such project. When producer Noah "40" Shebib heard that Diane Haughton had said, "I don't want this out", he walked away and the album was scuttled.

Even as that mini-tempest was brewing, Chris Brown, who had just won a Grammy Award for Best R&B Album for 2011 with F.A.M.E., was filming a music video for the song "Don't Think They Know." The song had originally been recorded as a duet between Aaliyah and Digital Black, then a member of Playa, in 2001. Black ultimately used the version on his "Memoirs of a R&B Thug" album in 2005. Aaliyah appears dancing in a hologram that was created from her videos in "Try Again" and If Your Girl Only Knew."

Michael Haughton would not be around to fight the fight to keep his daughter's memory from being appropriated by outsiders. He died in 2012, and was laid to rest in the Ferncliff Mausoleum next to Aaliyah. Michael and Diane Haughton had moved to White Plains, New York after Aaliyah had graduated high school so as to be close to their daughter.

The next affront to Aaliyah's memory came with the announcement that the cable network Lifetime was planning a biopic for release in the fall of 2014 entitled *Aaliyha: Princess of R&B*. Lifetime has built a reputation over creating unauthorized celebrity biography movies, and never saw fit to contact the Haughtons on any aspect of their daughter's story. Even if the family had been consulted, they likely would have been despondent about the proposed project, as they envisioned Aaliyah's story being told on the big screen "by a big-name studio with A-list stars."

Things did not improve when Disney star Zendaya Coleman was cast to play Aaliyah. While some questioned her acting and singing chops, others wondered if the half-black Zendaya looked the part of a hip hop icon. Zendaya shortly dropped out of the part, citing shoddy production values and problems with rights over the music controlled by Blackground and the Haughton family. She was replaced by 23-year old Alexandra Shipp, a Nickelodeon channel actress.

Chapter 8: Legacy

James Dean made three movies before he died in a motorcycle accident at 24. Buddy Holly made three albums before he died in a plane crash at 22. Aaliyah made three albums and two movies before she died in a plane crash at 22. Sometimes you do not need to sink that many pillars upon which to build a legend that will impact others that follow. All had profound influences on the artists that followed.

It would be hard to imagine the careers of Rihanna, Ciara, Ashanti, Beyoncé and more without Aaliyah. The one they called Baby Girl effortlessly conquered music, the movies and fashion in setting the standard for entertainment superstardom for young women in the 21st century. She lives on in their careers, but with the passage of time she belongs more and more to history.

Despite a singing career that lasted only three albums and fewer than 50 songs, you can find Aaliyah listed by *Billboard* as the 27th most successful rhythm and blues artist of all time. The music video channel VH1 ranks her number 48 on its list of "Greatest Women in Music." Her individual albums all slot somewhere into somebody's list of the best R&B albums of all time. She has sold more than 52 million records worldwide. And she managed to do it with music that sounds as fresh as when it was released two decades ago.

It is not that she ever set out to try and make an important record; that is a concept at odds with her lasting image of fun. Her first album was virtually all under the guidance of her mentor R. Kelly. She went in a different direction on her next album with the then-unknown Timbaland and Missy Elliott because she liked their sound; on her third outing, she sought new producers and sounds that she wanted to produce.

There was never a grand plan to shake up rhythm and blues; when the urban music world was moving toward hip hop soul, Aaliyah was leading the times, not following trends. There was never a plan to look hip hop-centered on stage; Aaliyah made it cool because that was how she dressed. There was never a plan to sell herself to the public as the girl-next-door while honing a streetwise edge - "street but sweet" was who she was, not a cynical marketing campaign. And for those who followed her, being genuine was the most important lesson.

Jorge Saralegui, the producer of *Queen of the Damned*, summed up what the movie professionals on set thought of her work when he said, "Aaliyah arrived in Melbourne extremely well-prepared and delivered a performance that will make everyone who loves her proud. She never complained about anything, including how long it took to dress and make her up. She was an actor who became famous as a singer and that puts her in the same company as, for example, Frank Sinatra and Cher, who delivered more than one critically lauded performance."

Just before her death, with both her acting and singing career locked in overdrive, Aaliyah was asked if she envisioned a day when she have to ultimately choose to follow a film career or a music career. "I hope not," she replied. "I want the public to look at me as an entertainer so I don't have to choose, especially not right now. I really just want to do it all." In history's eye, she never will have to choose.

Bibliography

Bogdanov, Vladimir; *All Music Guide to Soul: The Definitive Guide to R&B and Soul*, San Francisco, California: Backbeat Books, 2003.

Bailey, Peter; *Ebony*, "Gladys Knight: A New Love, A New Life," March 1975.

Farley, Christopher John; *Time*, "Aaliyah: More Than a Woman," December 8, 2001.

Gimenes, Erika; *Hollywood.com*, Aaliyah's family plans private funeral in New York," August 30, 2001.

Grow, Kory; *Rolling Stone*, "Drake and Noah '40' Shebib Call Off Posthumous Aaliyah Album," January 8, 2014.

Horowitz, Stephen J.; *Billboard Biz*, "Exclusive: Drake, Missy, Timbaland? Blackground Clarifies Rumors Swirling Around Aaliyah Album (Update)," August 9, 2012.

Kaye, Ken; *Sun Sentinel*, "Overloaded Plane Caused Aaliyah Crash, NTSB Says," September 9, 2001.

Kim, Hyun; *Vibe*, "What Lies Beneath," August 2001.

Fennessey, Sean; *Vibe*, "An Indecent Proposal," May 2007.

Maeder, Jay; *Big Town, Big Time: A New York Epic: 1898-1998*, New York City, New York: New York Daily News.

Reynolds, J.R.; *Billboard*, "Power Jam Focuses on Self-Improvement," March 2, 1996.

Siemaszko, Corky; *New York Daily News*, "Aaliyah's family wants big screen biopic with A-list star portraying late singer, not low-budget Lifetime TV movie," June 24, 2014.

Silverman, Stephen M.; *People*, "Aaliyah Remembered One Year Later," August 26, 2002.

Smith, Paul; *Jet*, "Sultry Singer Aliyah On Why It is So Cool to Be Hot," July 23, 2001.

Smolowe, Jill; *People*, "The Saddest Song," September 10, 2001.

Wadler, Joyce; *The New York Times*, "Private Mass, Public Tribute for Singer," September 1, 2001.

Young, Graham; *Birmingham Mail*, "Film: Aaliyah Live in Amsterdam - exclusive premiere," July 22, 2011.

Made in United States
Troutdale, OR
12/21/2023

16238651R10080